Praying with the Church:

An Introduction
to Prayer in Daily Life

Philip H. Pfatteicher

Augsburg Fortress
Minneapolis

For Carl and Linda, Doctors of Law,
and for their godchild Kelsey Elizabeth McDermott

PRAYING WITH THE CHURCH: An Introduction to Prayer in Daily Life

Scripture texts are from the New Revised Standard Version Bible, copyright 1989 by the Division of Christian Education of the National Council of the Churches of Christ in the United States of America. Used with permission.
Cover art: stained glass, Redeemer Lutheran Church, St. Paul, Minnesota
Cover design: Circus Design
Interior Design: Darwin Holmstrom

Library of Congress Cataloging-in-Publication Data

Pfatteicher, Philip H.
    Praying with the church: an introduction to prayer in daily life/Philip H. Pfatteicher.
    Includes bibliographical references.
    ISBN 0-8066-2805-7 (alk. paper)
    1. Divine office. 2. Prayer—Christianity. I. Title.
BV199.D3P43 1995
248.3'2—dc20   95-2091
                                                                       CIP

The Paper used in this publication meets the minimum requirements of American National Standard for Information Sciences—Permanence of Paper for Printed Library Materials, ANSI Z329.48-1984.

Manufactured in the U.S.A.

00 99 98 97 96 95 1 2 3 4 5 6 7 8 9 10

Contents

The abbreviations used in indicating the sources of quotations in this book are these:

BCP: *The Book of Common Prayer* according to the use of The Episcopal Church. New York: Church Hymnal Corporation, 1979.

CP: *Christian Prayer: The Liturgy of the Hours.* New York: Catholic Book Publishing Company, 1976.

H82: *The Hymnal 1982* according to the use of The Episcopal Church. New York: Church Hymnal Corporation, 1985.

LBW: *Lutheran Book of Worship.* Minneapolis and Philadelphia: Augsburg Publishing House and the Board of Publication, Lutheran Church in America, 1978.

LW: *Luther's Works.* American Edition. St. Louis and Philadelphia: Concordia Publishing House and Muhlenberg/Fortress Press, 1955–1986. 55 vols. (Cited as volume:page)

SBH: *Service Book and Hymnal.* Minneapolis and Philadelphia: Augsburg Publishing House and the Board of Publication, Lutheran Church in America, 1958.

WA: *D. Martin Luthers Werke.* Kritische Gesammtausgabe, J.K.F. Knaake *et al.,* eds. Weimar: Böhlau, 1883–.

Biblical quotations, except where otherwise noted, are from the New Revised Standard Version.

Psalm numbers are in accordance with the Hebrew/Protestant system; readers accustomed to the Roman Catholic/Orthodox numbering will need to make adjustments.

Preface

The understanding of prayer outlined in the following pages represents nearly half a century of thought, reflection, and practice. The first article I published was on the divine office. My doctoral dissertation examined the life and writings of a quiet and attractive figure who devised an immensely popular form of the breviary, John Austin (1613–1669). Since my undergraduate days I have constantly been at work on the development of a useful and practical version of the Daily Prayer of the Church in the evangelical catholic tradition. I have tried praying the Psalter by itself. I have supplemented that by daily reading of the Bible, a chapter or two a day. Though the Roman Breviary is quite complicated for individual devotional use, *The Book of Common Prayer,* with its complete Psalter arranged for monthly reading and a carefully chosen daily lectionary, has been helpful. I have used with profit *The Daily Office* compiled by the admirable pastor, Herbert Lindemann; but, with the far-reaching reforms outlined in the documents of the Second Vatican Council influencing the work of many denominations, this book is now out of date as well as out of print. The *Minister's Prayer Book,* compiled by my teacher John Doberstein, has a most useful anthology of readings on the work of the ministry; it is, however, intended primarily for clergy. Over the course of many decades, therefore, I have made my own revision and adaptation of the traditional daily prayer of the church as given in *Lutheran Book of Worship,* forthcoming from American Lutheran Publishing Bureau as *The Daily Prayer of the Church.* There one may see how the ideas presented in this essay are worked out in a reasonably complete book of prayer.

More people than I can number have contributed to my understanding and practice of prayer. Among them was Brian Helge

(1944–1991). I greatly regret that he, who worked with me and others in preparing the forms of Daily Prayer for *Lutheran Book of Worship,* could no longer sing the songs of Zion with us on our pilgrimage. He drafted the Lutheran version of Evening Prayer for *Lutheran Book of Worship,* and that office stands as his memorial. *Requiem aeternam dona ei, Domine. Et lux perpetua luceat ei.*

The past is important prologue, and prayer joins a long development with a bold and confident drive into the future. The dedication of this book is to my son and youngest daughter, a gift of generations past to generations yet to come.

I am grateful to Grace Church, Malverne, Long Island, New York and to its pastors, Thomas Eifert and Harvey von Harten, who twice invited me to lead assisting ministers of that parish and the region in a day of reflection and a discussion of some of the concerns elaborated in chapter 6 of this book.

Introduction

It has been wisely observed that what the church needs most is not more Christians but better Christians. The important questions have to do not with size but with quality: what does the church have to teach those who have been gathered? High on the list, surely, is an urgent need for guidance in the life of prayer, especially in an age in which prayer is no longer a common or familiar activity.

A proper understanding of prayer does not pull people more and more into themselves, as if what has often been called "the interior life" is a life in a house with the blinds shut and the curtains drawn, closing off the outside world. Authentic prayer takes place in the deepest recesses of one's being, but it is finally not one's own doing, nor is it one's own voice that is heard. Prayer, as St. Paul, Martin Luther, and other great teachers have known, is the work of the Spirit of God breathing within us. That breath, from the outside, is a constant challenge to us, inspiring us to move and to grow. Such developing maturity draws us into an ever-deeper relationship with God. At the same time, however, it necessarily draws us into an ever-deeper relationship with the world that God has made and with everyone and, indeed, with everything in that world.

As we pray, we need to listen to the voice of God within us, and we also need to listen to the voices and words of holy people of past centuries who have walked this way before us. Their words, their formulations, their discoveries can help us on our way in our time.

The accumulated wisdom is available in the traditional and classic collection of words and forms arranged in a cycle of prayer that has been known by various names. It is perhaps best of all described as the Daily Prayer of the Church: the prayer not just of individuals, but of the community, principally in the evening and in the morning, as the sun sets and as the sun rises, sometimes supplemented by prayer at other times of the day as well. This ordered devotion is also called the Liturgy of the Hours, prayer at stated times throughout the day by which the passage of time is opened to proclaim the basic declarations of the Christian faith. It is sometimes called the Daily Office (from the Latin *officium:* duty, obligation, service), for it is the daily duty and service of Christians willingly, even gladly, offered. It has been called the Divine Office, for this duty and obligation puts us in touch with the work of God. Regular, ordered prayer is our offering in praise of God, but as our prayer is offered not only *through* Christ but *with* Christ, the Redeemer who "always lives to make intercession" for us (Heb. 7:25). Our prayer becomes not only our doing but God's own work (*opus Dei,* St. Benedict called it). Offered in union with Christ, our prayer is the work of God in which we are invited to join.

The following pages are a recommendation of the use of the ancient way of Daily Prayer as a form to shape our spiritual life and to assist in our continuing Christian formation. This being our shared heritage, the discussion is addressed to all Christians, the concerned and thoughtful reader of any denominational tradition. Footnotes have been avoided to make this little volume less formidable.

To recommend the practice of following the Daily Prayer of the Church as the third millennium begins is, of course, to fly in the face of the prevailing view, which sets aside the past, revels in diversity, and holds religion as an intensely personal and private enterprise. The Daily Prayer of the Church is, nonetheless, a gift of great value to the present from centuries of Christian tradition, and it is what the world desperately needs to hear and learn. Only a large sense of the wholeness of time, humanity, and creation can give the solid grounding and the challenge to grow that the work of God requires.

I

....

With the Whole People of God

Prayer may seem a lonely activity. When gladness overflows we are moved to spontaneous praise; a thank-you of gratitude rises for God's goodness to *me*, sometimes at the expense of others. Perhaps more clearly, however, prayer is lonely when we cry out in deep anguish. We lose a job; a marriage is on the verge of ruin; a parent or, worse, a child dies. We may spend hours alone, wrestling with the collapse of hopes and dreams, coming to terms with the failure of promise. In such grim times no one seems able to share our personal sorrow. We struggle with a decision—what to do with our life, whether to accept or reject an offer—and no one can make the choice for us. We may not be praying people, but sometimes, when grief or trouble comes, we at least verge on prayer as we ponder deeply life's meaning and purpose.

The truth is, however, that we never pray alone. When, whether voluntarily or involuntarily, we begin to enter that strange and disconcerting temple we call prayer, we join with multitudes of others who share similar lonely crises, and we find that we are not alone after all. We are part of a community that shares in the blessings given through Holy Baptism.

Looking closer, we find first that God is present even in our darkest moments. The covenant given at our baptism establishes a permanent and irrevocable relationship between God and us. In the Lutheran baptismal rite, at the signing of the candidate with the cross, the presiding minister says with remarkable boldness, "Child of God, you have been sealed by the Holy Spirit and marked with the cross of Christ forever." (The language of the Episcopal rite is comparable.) God's love and calm are eternal. Martin Luther, in his splendid essay *The Holy and Blessed Sacrament of Baptism,* gave the consolation, "This blessed sacrament of baptism helps you because in it God allies himself with you and becomes one with you in a gracious covenant of comfort" (*LW* 35:33). When we feel abandoned, there is God the Creator and Redeemer beside us, waiting to hear and respond to our prayer. No place on earth is void of the divine presence. As St. Paul asserts in that ringing declaration of confidence in Romans 8,

> I am convinced that neither death, nor life, nor angels, nor rulers, nor things present, nor things to come, nor powers, nor height, nor depth, nor anything else in all creation, will be able to separate us from the love of God in Christ Jesus our Lord.

Second, when we pray we find what St. Paul calls the sharing of Christ's sufferings (Phil. 3:10). Indeed, we willingly take on the power of the resurrection and the sharing of Christ's sufferings, for one is incomplete without the other. Luther calls suffering and death "the work of baptism," and says that "in the easy life no one learns to suffer, to die with gladness, to get rid of sin, and to live in harmony with baptism" (*LW* 35:39). A 19th century Lutheran confirmation formula has it exactly right: "The Father in Heaven, for Jesus' sake, renew and increase in thee the gift of the Holy Ghost, to thy strengthening in faith, to thy growth in grace, *to thy patience in suffering,* and to the blessed hope of everlasting life." The church's prayer for those it confirms is for growth, and growth in a fallen world must inescapably include suffering. It is, however, more than the common observation that suffering is sometimes unavoidable. Baptism, and thus prayer, draw us into Christ's suffering, that strange and mysterious communion of those who willingly, even gladly, accept redemption and redemptive activity; and who, following the example of their Lord, take on themselves the pain of the world.

Third, bound by our baptism to the sufferings and to the resurrection of Christ, we receive in prayer the consolation of the Holy Spirit, our Advocate and Guide. Holy Baptism gives us the Spirit of God as our constant companion, defender, and leader, who prays within us (Rom. 26–27).

More than that, those who have been joined to God by baptism have been joined to a vast company that no one can number, those who have gone before us through this sometimes grim and perplexing world. The saints of God, holy men and women whose memory we celebrate as examples for our journey, are like us; and the hope is that we can be like them. We are part of that great multitude, united by our participation in the sacrament of Christ's body and blood.

Whoever is in despair, distressed, or carrying some burden on the heart, says Luther, let that person "go joyfully to the sacrament of the altar and lay down his woe in the midst of the community [of saints] and seek help from the entire company of the spiritual body" (*LW* 35:53). God gives us the sacrament of the holy supper as if to say, "Look, many kinds of sin are assailing you; take this sign by which I give you my pledge that this sin is assailing not only you but also my Son, Christ, and all his saints in heaven and on earth. Therefore take heart and be bold. You are not fighting alone. Great help and support are all around you" (*LW* 35:53).

Having received that support, it is the duty and obligation of the recipients to extend it to others.

> When you have partaken of this sacrament, therefore, or desire to partake of it, you must in turn share the misfortunes of the fellowship. … As love and support are given you, you in turn must render love and support to Christ and his needy ones. You must feel with sorrow all the dishonor done to Christ and his holy Word, all the misery of Christendom, all the unjust suffering of the innocent, with which the world is everywhere filled to overflowing. You must fight, work, pray, and—if you cannot do more—have heartfelt sympathy (*LW* 35:54)

Prayer quickens our conscience and leads us out of ourselves to solidarity with the whole church. The church on earth is one, and its communion with God and with one another increases the desire of its communicants to share the sufferings of others.

Indeed we may believe that all heaven—all the angels and all the saints already in glory—are praying for us on earth, the church triumphant in heaven confidently praying for the church militant in its earthly struggles. Even death is no barrier to the unity and communal concern of God's people.

At times we long to join the number of those whose course is finished. Like Christian at the end of John Bunyan's *Pilgrim's Progress* as the gates open to receive pilgrims, through prayer we get a brief look into heaven. What we see, what is promised, is more than we can imagine, and we would like to be there now. But, as the last paragraph of *Pilgrim's Progress* teaches, we cannot yet enter that holy city. We have the remainder of our life to live first, and mingled with the joy and fulfillment God grants us is continued watchfulness, temptation, struggle, and effort. What gives us courage to continue is the knowledge that others before us have remained faithful and that we are already part of their number. For, as St. John suggests, eternal life is not only a hope for sometime in the future; it is a present possession.

Essential to our solidarity with that communion of saints are frequent reminders of the size and nature of the church of God. To nourish, enliven, and give us living participation we need prayer. For prayer deepens our relationship with God and with the church.

When we pray we are never alone. We join with others who pray now and who lead lives of prayer and communion with God, and we also join with those of all times and all places who have walked this way before us. Prayer is never an individual, isolated activity. Even when we struggle alone in the darkness, abandoned by all around us, perhaps even by our family, even then, whether we are aware of it or not, we pray as part of a tradition that is wide and diverse, and in our lonely struggle that larger dimension may be revealed to us. We are not, after all, isolated. We learn that we are part of the company of God's faithful people. Ignatius of Antioch (d. ca. 115) urged in his letter to the Ephesians, "Try to gather together more frequently to celebrate God's Eucharist and to praise him"(ch. 13). In the next century Cyprian of Carthage in Africa (d. 258) sharpened the observation: "The Lord of unity did not command that prayer be offered to him individually and in private" (*On the Lord's Prayer* 8). In the ancient church, times of public, gathered prayer seem clearly to have been understood as something necessary, and indeed superior to private prayer.

There is an old tradition in the church that when one prays the Liturgy of the Hours alone, before the collect of the day, instead of saying, "The Lord be with you" and answering oneself, "And also with you," one says rather the verse from Psalm 39:12, "Hear my prayer, O LORD,/And give ear to my cry." It seems an eminently sensible practice, aimed at making the words mean something. Yet when we pray alone, we do not pray in isolation from the community of faith. As there is no such thing as "private communion," because the Holy Communion is always the communion with God and with the church at which all the company of heaven are present, so there can be no such thing as private prayer.

Such a view does not threaten the importance of individual prayer apart from stated times of the gathered assembly. Rather, it deepens our understanding of what we do apparently by ourselves, revealing depths and dimensions that we may not have been aware. We have more company than we thought; we have more support than we imagined. Elisha prayed for his servant whose faith was too small, "O LORD, open his eyes that he may see" (2 Kings 6:15–17). And the servant of the prophet of God saw the entire mountain filled with angelic armies. Elisha's prayer is not only for his servant; it is also for us. The people of the new covenant pray in the name of Jesus, who promised that "where two or three are gathered in my name, I am there among them" (Matt. 18:20). The familiar promise is not so much a comfort to those groups whose numbers are small as an urging to gather with others to pray in community as the expression and realization of the body of Christ, shown and confessed by their very assembly. St. Paul warns the Corinthian church against participating in the Eucharist "without discerning the body" (1 Cor. 11:29). This passage has often been understood to state the necessity of affirming the "real presence" of Christ's body and blood in the sacramental elements of bread and wine; it is perhaps better understood as a warning against individualism. When we receive the sacrament, we are bound to the whole body of Christ, and worthy reception requires that we recognize our solidarity with the community. The same holds true for our participation in prayer.

Prayer is not only our *privilege* as the baptized people of God, enabled to call upon God who has adopted us into the chosen family, but it is our *responsibility* as well, our solemn duty and obligation as members, constituent parts of Christ's body. The *Apostolic Constitutions,* a church order written at Antioch ca. 380, warns:

> Do not scatter yourselves (Matt. 12:30), who are members of Christ, by not assembling together, since you have Christ as your head, according to his promise, present and communicating to you (Matt. 28:20). Do not be careless and deprive your Savior of his own members, not divide his body nor disperse his members nor prefer the occasions of this world to the Word of God; but assemble yourselves together every day, morning and evening, singing psalms and praying in the Lord's house. (7.59)

Our absence from the assembly weakens the community and lets down the other members. Our neglect of prayer lessens the wholeness of the prayer of the people of God, that mighty throng whose prayer thunders against the enemy and rises like incense to the throne of God. Luther insisted:

> This sacrament of fellowship, love, and unity cannot tolerate discord and disunity. You must take to heart the infirmities and needs of others, as if they were your own. Then offer to others your strength, as if it were their own, just as Christ does for you in the sacrament. This is what it means to be changed into one another through love, out of many particles to become one bread and drink, to lose one's own form and take on that which is common to all. (*LW* 35:61–2)

Luther apparently unwittingly echoes that wonderful prayer in the late-first or early-second century church order, the *Didache* (not discovered until 1873): "As this piece [of bread] was scattered over the hills and then was brought together and made one, so let your church be brought together from the ends of the earth into your Kingdom" (*LW* 9:4).

The familiar dichotomy between private and public prayer is, therefore, fundamentally mistaken. We cannot sit back and let others do all the praying for us, but neither can we do it all by ourselves. Christians pray as members of the body of Christ, enabled by baptism and the gift of the Spirit to pray as children in God's family and to call God Father. Their prayer is sealed with the "Amen," and that mighty affirmation reminds us "that the whole of Christendom, all devout Christians, are standing there beside [us] and [we] are standing among them in a common, united petition which God cannot disdain" (*LW* 43:198). Our prayer is the church's prayer, and the church's prayer is our prayer.

2

....

What Language Shall We Borrow?

As we try to pray we are confronted by the magnitude of the enterprise and the meagerness of our resources. We find we do not have the words; we do not even understand our experience and so cannot lay it before God. We want to pray, but we find that we cannot do it on our own. The deeper we get into prayer the less satisfactory our own words and feelings seem. We need help. If prayer is an encounter with the Holy God, how dare we flawed mortal people approach the fountain of all holiness? What claim have we on the attention of God who supports and sustains the universe? When we tremblingly enter that daunting presence, with what words do we come, what are we to say?

Much of the prayer we hear around us is not much help. We watch preachers on television screwing their eyes closed with a pained expression to mouth platitudes and favorite phrases remote from real experience. If we listen to such "free" prayers regularly we find that they vary very little. Their freedom is an illusion. The phrases are the same, over and over, still floating past us without making connection.

Trapped between a naive biblicism on one hand and a widespread disregard of religion on the other, what are we to do when we are moved to pray or to cry out in pain? What language can we find? What are we to say?

Our own creativity is inadequate. A translation of Paul Gerhardt's moving passion hymn, "O Sacred Head, Now Wounded," has us ask the dying Savior, "What language can I borrow to thank thee, dearest friend?"

The opening versicle and response of Morning Prayer recognizes our dilemma and suggests a solution: "O Lord, open my lips/And my mouth will declare your praise" (Ps. 51:15). Even as we seek to turn to God in prayer, it is God who helps us give voice to that which wells up within us. Indeed, when our attempts at praying seem utterly to fail, still God comes to our aid:

> Likewise the Spirit helps us in our weakness; for we do not know how to pray as we ought, but that very Spirit intercedes with sighs too deep for words. And God, who searches the heart, knows what is the mind of the Spirit, because the Spirit intercedes for the saints according to the will of God.
>
> (Rom. 8:26–27)

Nevertheless, we need to put our deep feelings into words, yet often cannot find the right words. Where then do we turn? There is abundant help available, if we know where to look. Of the accumulated experience and wisdom of centuries of prayer by a variety of people in a variety of places and in a variety of situations, a residue has survived. Tested, refined, distilled from the experience of those who knew most about prayer through many centuries, a treasury has been accumulated, and it is available to us. We are free to borrow that language. Indeed, often the best language to express to God our anguish or concern, our praise or thanksgiving comes not from our own mind or creativity. It is borrowed from others who are better poets than we are, more experienced in prayer, more accustomed to praise. It is borrowed from the treasury of prayer gathered through the centuries, an invaluable collection available for the use of others who follow.

A gifted individual can create a work of surpassing beauty. That creation is an enduring individual achievement. Everyone knows Leonardo da Vinci's *Last Supper,* Michelangelo's *Pietà,* Philipp Nicolai's "O Morning Star, How Fair and Bright." But ordinary people in the course of time can create works of art, too. In English literary history the "popular ballads" (that is, ballads created by the people) are such achievements. A story is put into verse or song by an unknown author. As the song passes through decades and even centuries, it is shaped and edited and refined in the process of transmission so that only the essential details remain. All extraneous information and material is removed. The result is a highly concentrated and powerful song that tells us what we need to know for maximum impact. The irrelevant having been pruned away, what remains is exactly what we need to hear, no more, no less.

A biblical example of such a song is the strange and terrifying Song of Deborah (Judges 5) celebrating the fall of an enemy commander at the hands of a woman, Jael. A song is put into the mouth of Deborah, the judge and prophet; the song is of a woman's victory and its impact not only on Israel but on the enemy's mother whose son lies dead with a tent peg through his skull. The women—wives, mothers, and other relatives of the defeated army—wait for their men to return. As too much time passes they grow restless. Sisera's mother tries to console herself by imagining that her son's triumph was so great that it is taking an unusually long time to divide the spoil, all the while afraid that it is a lie. We never hear how she learned of her son's death or what her reaction was; we do not need to. The ancient song is stronger because it allows us to imagine ourselves as Sisera's mother and what the dreaded news would do to us. The last verses of the song, far from undercutting the power of the triumph, deepen our understanding of this and any military victory. We cannot simply cheer mindlessly for the victorious side. Some die; some mothers are left childless by the war. The implications are more complex than we might like. Superfluous explanations are stripped away, and only the essential core remains full of power and enhanced force.

Though such fine-tuned songs are found throughout the Bible, the richest collection of "right words" for prayer is the Book of Psalms. These mostly anonymous Iron Age songs were shaped and refined through centuries of use until they reached a permanent and enduring form that can still speak to a technological world at the beginning of the twenty-first century. They have endured because they retain their ancient power. We who may know so little about prayer and about our own experience, who have trouble finding words can borrow from the psalms their insight and their language.

The psalms are the core of Daily Prayer. Many of the unchanging parts of Daily Prayer in *Lutheran Book of Worship,* for example, are drawn from psalms—in Morning Prayer, "Oh, come, let us sing to the LORD . . ." (Ps. 95); in Evening Prayer, "Let my prayer be counted as incense before you . . ." (Ps. 141); in Prayer at the Close of the Day, "It is good to give thanks to the LORD . . ." (Ps. 92). In addition, each prayer service requires that additional psalms be sung or said. As we explore their riches, these ancient and yet ever-new songs help us find our voice. Athanasius (d. 373) declared in a letter to Marcellinus that

The Lord, wishing the melody of the words to be a symbol of the spiritual harmony of the soul, has ordered that the odes be chanted tunefully, and the Psalms be recited with song. The desire of the soul is this—to be beautifully disposed, as it is written, "Are any among you cheerful? They should sing songs of praise" (James 5:13). In this way that which is disturbing and rough and disorderly is smoothed away, and that which causes grief is healed when we sing psalms. (Letter 28)

Psalms, when prayed, become our own prayer. John Cassian (ca. 360–ca. 435) reports that the early monks did not seem so much to be reciting the psalms as to be recreating them, for they sang them from the heart as if they were extempore prayers. Indeed, as Athanasius says, "The one who hears is deeply moved, as though he himself were speaking, and is affected by the words of the songs, as if they were his own songs" (Letter 11).

We do not treat any other part of the Bible this way, not the words of the patriarchs, not the preaching of the prophets. Each of us sings the psalms "as if they were written concerning us," Athanasius wrote.

> The Psalms are not recited with melodies out of a desire for pleasant sounds. The melody is instead a sure sign of the harmony of the soul's reflections. Indeed, the melodic reading is a symbol of a well-ordered and undisturbed mind. Moreover, the praising of God in well-tuned cymbals and harps and ten-stringed instruments was an image and sign of the parts of the body coming into natural concord like harp strings, and of the thoughts of the soul becoming like cymbals, and then all these being moved and living through the grand sound and through the command of the Spirit so that, as it is written, those who live in the Spirit mortify the deeds of the body (Rom. 8:1:13). For thus beautifully singing praises, they bring rhythm to their souls and lead them, so to speak, from disproportion to proportion. . . . (Letter 29)

These ancient songs have endured through the ages because generations upon generations have found in them a window on the lives that God intends for his people. Luther called the Psalter "a little Bible" and said of it,

> Other books make much ado about the works of the saints, but say very little about their words. The Psalter is a gem in this respect. . . . It presents to us not the simple ordinary

speech of the saints, but the best of their language, that which they used when they talked with God himself in great earnestness and on the most important matters. . . . There you look into the hearts of all the saints, as into fair and pleasant gardens, yes, as into heaven itself.

The Psalter holds you to the communion of saints and away from the sects. For it teaches you in joy, fear, hope, and sorrow to think and speak as all the saints have thought and spoken.

In a word, if you would see the holy Christian Church painted in living color and shape, comprehended in one little picture, then take up the Psalter. (*LW* 35:254–257)

The Psalter makes God's people in the past alive to us, giving us insight into how their hearts were conditioned, and it enables us to hear how they spoke with God and with others. Not all of it is to be emulated. We might wish that the terrible words of Psalm 109 were not there. Such emotions are, we think, surely better left unspoken, unthought. Yet they are feelings we do sometimes have, and honesty requires that we acknowledge and confront such reprehensible attitudes.

Iron Age songs may at first seem remote from our experience and difficult for modern people to get hold of. They do require careful and sustained attention. Their use within Daily Prayer can be enriched by using antiphons—usually a verse from the Bible—before and after the psalm to set that psalm in a seasonal context. A breviary provides the most complete selection of such antiphons. In the one-volume edition of the Roman Catholic Liturgy of the Hours, Psalm 110:1–5, 7 is used in Evening Prayer II for several festivals, but the antiphons help bring out different nuances. For Epiphany, the antiphon compares Christ to mortal kings: "He comes in splendor, the King who is our peace; he is supreme over all the kings of the earth" (CP 214). For use on Easter Sunday, the antiphon for the same psalm is "Mary Magdalene and the other Mary came to see the Lord's tomb, alleluia" (CP 429). While not containing as extensive a selection as single- or multi-volume breviaries, *Lutheran Book of Worship* (pp. 174–177) and *The Book of Common Prayer* (pp. 43–44, 80–82) do provide some psalm antiphons.

Moreover, in some traditions each psalm is followed by a psalm prayer that draws out the meaning of the psalm as it is used in Christian worship, adding insights drawn from the New Testament. The words of the psalm retain their integrity but are given increased richness and dimension by the prayer. (These psalm prayers are located, following their respective psalms, in the *LBW: Minister's Desk Edition* , pp. 340 ff.)

Each individual can find in the psalms the words needed to see what it means to be a Christian. Thus the Psalter teaches that prayer is the heart's conversation with God and reminds us of the unity between the Old and the New Testaments and the fact that the whole Bible is God's Word to us. Finding our own words in the psalms, we learn how we may find our place in the whole biblical story and how that ancient story becomes our story.

The psalms are at the heart of Daily Prayer, but they are not the only part of the Bible that has a place in the traditional forms of ordered prayer. The Gospel canticles—Magnificat, the song of Mary (Luke 1:46–55); Benedictus, the song of Zechariah (Luke 1:68–79); and Nunc Dimittis, the song of Simeon (Luke 2:29–32)—occupy an important place in the services of Daily Prayer. The first two are also given antiphons to highlight a phrase for that day or to join them to the celebration of a festival. (See LBW pp. 174–177.) Some antiphons are taken from the Bible; others are independent liturgical compositions. These brief antiphons, though, pale before more elaborate ones developed over the centuries. The Magnificat antiphon for the Feast of the Epiphany (January 6), as provided in the Roman Catholic breviary, may serve as an example.

> Three mysteries mark this holy day:
> today the star leads the Magi
> to the infant Christ;
> today water is changed into wine
> for the wedding feast;
> today Christ wills to be baptized
> by John in the river Jordan
> to bring us salvation.   (*CP* 216)

The ancient triple celebration of the feast day is recalled and renewed: the Epiphany is a three-fold celebration of the adoration of the Magi, the first miracle that Jesus performed changing water into wine at Cana in Galilee, and Jesus' acceptance of baptism by John. All this was done to bring us salvation.

The lectionary for Daily Prayer provides regular daily support for individual or corporate meditation on scripture and satisfies the ancient desire for continuous reading of the Bible for instruction and devotion. The psalms provide us with words which we are invited to use, to grow into, the make our own. In the biblical lessons we listen to God's Word addressed to us. We do so not alone and in private in a study, but in the context of the gathered assembly, of prayer, contemplation, and praise. In this way, reading and listening are united and do not remain an isolated event or an end in themselves. They are part of a larger act of offering as we render our praise and give ourselves to God for whatever further service may be required.

Following the lessons, at least at Morning Prayer, a responsory is traditional in the Roman Catholic and Lutheran use, though in *Lutheran Book of Worship* it is optional and so, often overlooked. Such responsories are choir pieces but also useful for meditation, composed usually of verses from the Bible, sometimes amplified, brought together and often ingeniously arranged so that Scripture is made to enlighten and comment on itself. A simple example is this responsory from "general" or "ordinary" time (the time after the Epiphany and after Pentecost) joining 2 Corinthians 8:9 and Philippians 2:7:

> You know the generous act of our Lord Jesus Christ,
> that though he was rich, yet for your sakes he became poor,*
>   so that by his poverty
>   you might become rich.
> He emptied himself, taking the form of a slave,*
>   so that by his poverty,
>   you might become rich.

A responsory for the Baptism of Our Lord, the First Sunday after the Epiphany, expands upon Psalm 114:5:

> Today the heavens opened*
> and the waters of the sea became sweet and fragrant.
> The earth rejoiced,
> the mountains and hills exulted*
>   because Christ was baptized by John in the Jordan.
> What ailed you, O sea, that you fled?
> O Jordan, that you turned back?*
>   Because Christ was baptized by John in the Jordan.

A responsory for Christmas Day uses rich poetic phrases echoing scriptural ideas and language but not specific citations:

Today true peace came down to us from heaven.*
Today the whole earth was filled with heaven's sweetness.
Today a new day dawns, the day of our redemption,
prepared by God from ages past,
the beginning of our never-ending gladness.*
Today the whole earth was filled with heaven's sweetness.

Such soaring song challenges our comfortable understandings of Christmas as a time for sentimental thoughts of peace and good will on earth and asserts the participation of the earth in the celebration of the Incarnation.

The richest, most complex, and most haunting of all the responsories in the church's treasury is perhaps the one for the first Sunday in Advent.

Watching from afar,*
I see the power of God coming,
and a cloud covering the whole earth.
Go out to meet him and say,*
Tell us if you are the one
who is to reign over your people Israel.
All people of the earth, all children of dust,
rich and poor alike,*
go out to meet him and say,
Shepherd of Israel, hear us,
you lead Joseph's race like a flock:*
Tell us if you are the one.

Open wide the gates, you princes,
let the King of glory enter,*
who is to come to reign over your people Israel.

Watching from afar,*
I see the power of God coming,
and a cloud covering the whole earth.
Go out to meet him and say,*
Tell us if you are the one
who is to reign over your people Israel.

The biblical allusions and echoes include Job 36:25; Jeremiah 30:10; 46:27; Ezekiel 38:9,16; Matthew 11:3; Micah 4:7; Psalms 49:2; 80:1; 24:7. It is a most moving plea.

The offices of Daily Prayer each conclude with explicit prayer. Such prayers, whether in the form of collects or litanies, turn the praise of Evensong and Morning Prayer to more specific activity. They formulate a response to the preceding praise and readings, finding words to clarify what the songs and readings mean to those who sing and hear them, declaring what worshipers, having joined such exalted activity, must now do. We ask for necessary gifts and graces to assist us in living a life of praise; we express how we are to conduct ourselves in response to our worship and adoration, for to enter into communion with God is to enter into a movement, to participate in a history that is nothing less than a history of God. Holiness, as Edmund Spenser demonstrates in the first book of the *Faerie Queen,* is an active virtue requiring not withdrawal from the world and its conflicts but unceasing combat with all that is hostile to God and virtue. The words of such prayers are simple and carefully chosen. The classic prayers of Christianity, the collects, are brief but pointed and abundantly suggestive. "The fewer the words, the better the prayer," observed Luther (LW 42:19). Such brevity is often characteristic of compelling literature, but it is especially true of the best prayers in the church's heritage.

Prayers written for Morning and Evening Prayer in *The Book of Common Prayer* have passed into wider Christian use. The General Thanksgiving formulates and teaches the appropriate response to the gifts that God has showered upon us:

> We bless you for our creation, preservation, and all the blessings of this life; but above all for your immeasurable love in the redemption of the world by our Lord Jesus Christ; for the means of grace, and for the hope of glory. And, we pray, give us such an awareness of your mercies, that with truly thankful hearts we may show forth your praise, not only with our lips, but in our lives, by giving up ourselves to your service, and by walking before you in holiness and righteousness all our days. (*BCP* 101, 125)

In *The Book of Common Prayer,* the *Prayer of St. Chrysostom* concludes the series of prayers.

> Almighty God, you have given us grace at this time with one accord to make our common supplication to you; and you have promised through your well-beloved Son that when two or three are gathered together in his Name you will be in the midst of them: Fulfill now, O Lord, our desires and petitions as may be best for us; granting us in this world knowledge of your truth, and in the age to come life everlasting. (*BCP* 102, 126)

The prayer elegantly submits to the good will of God, asking but one gift in this world and one in the world to come.

In the Roman Catholic and Lutheran orders, the prayers conclude with the Lord's Prayer, the simple but beautiful words our Savior taught us. In this way, we are not only reminded once more that we pray "*through* Jesus Christ our Lord" but that we are enabled by these hallowed phrases to pray *with* our high priest, representative, and intercessor. Our words join with his, and his pure and perfect intention more and more becomes ours.

Daily Prayer teaches valuable lessons in humility. In Daily Prayer we learn what is important and what is not, and we find our proper place in the grand cycle of cosmic praise, praying with our Lord, "not my will but yours be done." The treasury of prayer is thus more than a depository that we may draw upon as we choose. It is an effective means of sanctification.

3

A Heritage of Prayer

How did the various times and structures of Daily Prayer become established? In the time of Jesus, devout Jews—thrice daily, "Evening and morning and at noon" (Ps. 55:17)—would face toward Jerusalem and pray, thus linking their personal devotion to the daily public prayer in the holy city. In the temple, sacrifice and prayer were offered twice each day: at nine o'clock in the morning and at three o'clock in the afternoon (Exodus 29:39; 30:7–8). That basic pattern of prayer two or three times each day remained through the history of Israel and Judaism, and it passed into Christian practice as well. Indeed, prayer as night falls and prayer as the sun rises seem ingrained in the human spirit. As the light declines, the shadows lengthen, and the evening comes, it is natural to commend ourselves to God for safekeeping through the hours of darkness; and as the light returns with opportunity and promise and the sun rises in strength, it is natural to thank God for guarding us and to ask for help and guidance in our daily work. The New Testament suggests that the apostles continued the Jewish practice of prayer at the principal hours of the day: midnight (Psalm 119:62; Acts 16:25), the third hour or 9 A.M. by modern reckoning (Acts 2:15), noon (Acts 10:9), the ninth hour or 3 P.M. (Acts 3:1); see also Daniel 6:10; Psalms 34:1 119:164.

By the end of the second century, as Hippolytus in the *Apostolic Tradition* (41), Tertullian *On Prayer* (25), and Cyprian *On the Lord's Prayer* (34–35) testify, morning and evening prayers were taken for granted in many places and were perhaps even regarded as the norm. To these two basic hours that were perhaps times for public prayer, additional prayers were recommended at the third, sixth, and ninth hours. These times were sometimes explained by relating them to stages of the passion of Christ (the third hour when Christ was crucified and when the Spirit descended at Pentecost; the sixth hour when darkness descended on Good Friday; the ninth hour when Christ died on the cross) making each day a re-living of the work of salvation. A daily pattern emerged that enumerated six times of prayer each day—dawn, mid-morning, noon, mid-afternoon, evening, and midnight. Hippolytus also recommends prayer at cockcrow, thus urging prayer seven times a day.

By the fourth century there is evidence of a fully developed daily public prayer service in Jerusalem. The content of this early Christian daily prayer is not known, but it probably reflected the synagogue services and perhaps included psalmody, Bible reading and preaching, the Lord's Prayer, the Sanctus, reciting the Ten Commandments, a profession of faith, some prayers, and a blessing of God. Traces of the services may be reflected in the New Testament as in St. Paul's reference to "psalms, hymns, and spiritual songs" (Col. 3:16; Eph. 5:19), suggesting both old and new songs, biblical psalms, and hymns from sources other than the Bible.

As we know it, Daily Prayer is a combination of two different patterns of prayer. There was what has been called for convenience the *cathedral office* that developed from the non-eucharistic public prayer of the church, characterized by simplicity and a limited number of fixed psalms such as Psalm 63 and the "laudate psalms" (148–150) in the morning and 141 in the evening. In cathedrals and larger city churches the public services of psalms and prayers were apparently customary. The services were led by secular (that is, non-monastic) clergy.

There was also what was called the *monastic office,* developed in the fourth century as monasticism grew after Christianity was recognized in the Roman Empire. The monks' purpose was to give themselves to constant prayer; their duty (*officium,* hence "office") was to pray. The primary feature of the monastic office was the regular recitation of the entire Psalter over a given period of time (often one week) without reference to the hour of the day or the season.

Ultimately, to the principal hours of Lauds at sunrise and Vespers at sunset—which laity and ascetics alike attended—were added the "day hours" of prayer at mid-morning (Terce), at noon (Sext), and at mid-afternoon (None). Added in monasteries were Prime at the beginning of the work day and Compline at bedtime, as well as an office in the middle of the night (Matins or Nocturns). John Cassian, a westerner from Gaul who visited monasteries in Palestine and Egypt in the last decade of the fourth century, reports such practice. St. Basil of Caesarea (d. 379), whose writings became the foundation of Eastern monasticism, also recognized these eight hours of prayer. By combining two of the hours of prayer or by counting seven day hours plus nocturns these were often reckoned as seven hours to conform to Psalm 119:164, "seven times a day I praise you."

The elaborate monastic prayer was used by the few whose whole life was prayer. But, in this, monks represented signs of the calling and obligation of all Christians: to be people of prayer, whose lives are an offering of prayer and praise, whose every action is significant for time and eternity.

There were many varieties of the monastic office from monastery to monastery, but the office prescribed by the *Rule* of St. Benedict (d. 540) for his monastery at Monte Cassino, a revision of the practice in Rome, became as fundamental for monasteries in the West as Basil's was for the East. Benedict distributed the Psalter over one week: introduced the antiphonal style of singing the psalms (two groups singing verses of the psalms alternately) with an antiphon, usually taken from the psalm, sung before and after each; added the opening versicles ("O Lord, open my lips;/and my mouth will declare your praise" to begin Nocturns and "Make haste, O God, to deliver me;/make haste to help me, O Lord" to begin the other hours); added responses after the lessons; included hymns at all the hours; placed the Te Deum after the final lesson at Nocturns; set the Benedictus at Lauds and the Magnificat at Vespers followed by *preces* (Kyrie, Our Father, versicles). The services were sung in the choir of the church or abbey—between the nave and the chancel— and so were called the choir (in an English spelling, sometimes "quire") services.

In the West, the secular (non-monastic) clergy adapted the full course of daily prayer developed by the monks, and when Charlemagne imposed the Roman service books throughout his kingdom, the divine offices of Rome were required of all clergy assigned to cathedrals and parish churches. The old public cathedral office had disappeared.

By the ninth century Vigils (Nocturns) had twelve or eighteen psalms; Lauds had Psalms 51, 63, 67, and a daily variable psalms (5, 43, 65, 90, 143, 92, 100), a canticle, the Laudate Psalms (148–150), the Benedictus, a short reading, *preces* (Kyrie, Our Father, Apostles' Creed, Psalm 51, and fixed verses) and a collect; daytime prayer divided Psalm 119 throughout the week with Psalm 118 on Sundays and Psalm 54 on weekdays; Vespers added *preces* also; Compline was short and simple as befits bedtime prayer: three fixed psalms (4, 91, 134), versicle, and Nunc Dimittis. Psalms 1–109 were assigned to Nocturns, Psalms 110–147 to Vespers.

The work of Daily Prayer had become so complex that many books were necessary for its celebration: a Bible, a book of sermons called a homilary, a book of collects called the collector, a book of antiphons called the antiphonary, the Psalter, and the order of the services. An outline of the offices of the year called a breviary appeared as a summary and guide to the many necessary books. Into the outline of the breviary complete texts could be inserted. The lectionaries could not be included in a volume of manageable size, and so the lessons were greatly abbreviated to a verse or two but continued to be called the "chapter."

By the thirteenth century the daily prayer services ("Offices") of the papal chapel, reduced from their earlier complexity as the administration of the work of the pope's curia increased, became the basis for a revision of the Office. The papal office was basically clerical and monastic, with a highly complex calendar of added saints' days and octaves (the eighth day of a festival, one week later) and commemorations obscuring the Sunday and daily office, with an Office of the Dead and an Office of the Blessed Virgin added to the office of the day. It is hardly surprising to find that there was widespread dissatisfaction with the state of the Office.

Laypeople had their own version of the clerical Office, called on the continent the Book of Hours and in England the Primer. It consisted of the Creed, the Lord's Prayer, the Ten Commandments, the Gradual Psalms (the psalms of ascent, 120–134) and the Penitential Psalms (6, 32, 38, 51, 102, 130, 143), the Office of the Dead, the Little Office of Our Lady, and other devotions.

The Office had become enormously complex and for those who prayed it (almost exclusively the clergy) it was often received as a burden rather than as a joy. In 1535 the Spanish cardinal Francisco de Quiñones (1480–1540) was asked by Pope Clement VII to revise the breviary to emphasize the recitation of the Psalter every week and the reading of the entire new Testament in a year together with a great deal of the Old Testament. This revised Office, since it was designed for private use, suppressed many of the choral elements such as antiphons and responsories that gave the Office variety and interest. Quiñones' Office itself was suppressed in 1558.

By the dawn of the Reformation, the Office became a complicated and daunting burden. What a wonder it survived at all, when the emerging churches made fresh starts in so many other matters of church life. Luther's *Formula Missae* (1523) continued the use of Matins and Vespers; his *Deutsche Messe* (1526) reiterated the recommendation. The Lutheran church orders modified the Office and combined hours (Matins, Lauds, and Prime were combined and Vespers joined with elements of Compline) to fit them for daily public use as morning and evening services for preaching and instruction. The church orders kept the Latin Psalter, often with the old plainsong tones, assigning Psalms 1–109 to Matins and 110–150 to Vespers. But with the rise of vernacular hymnody the use of the Psalter was gradually undermined. Lutheran piety became more attuned to hymns than to psalms and often used hymn texts privately for personal meditation. Among Lutherans, appointed lessons for Matins and Vespers have generally been taken less seriously than the eucharistic lectionary, the eucharistic readings sometimes serving both for use at the Holy Communion and at Morning or Evening Prayer. In Lutheran lands, Matins and Vespers survived some years in academic settings, but their use eventually declined.

In England, following Luther and Quiñones, Thomas Cranmer simplified and combined the seven-fold Office into two, Morning and Evening Prayer. He removed all antiphons, responsories, hymns, and most versicles. The Psalter was sung in course each month (the Psalter in *The Book of Common Prayer* is still so marked for those who desire to continue the practice); the Old Testament was read through once a year, the New Testament twice a year. Later, a confession and an absolution were added to the beginning of the services and the prayers expanded. The Office became familiar to laity because of its use as a substitute for the Eucharist on Sunday morning in Anglican churches and because of the popularity of choral Evensong in English cathedrals with their renowned choirs. Moreover the expectation was that all clergy of the Church of England would pray Morning and Evening Prayer daily, in their parish churches if possible. The influence of these services went far beyond Anglicanism and in the nineteenth century became the norm of the weekly worship in many Protestant churches.

In the Lutheran confessional and liturgical revival in the latter half of the nineteenth century Matins and Vespers were restored to Lutheran use by reformers like Wilhelm Loehe in Bavaria. Parish schools and deaconess communities assisted in the recovery. A form of Vespers became a popular Sunday evening service toward the end of the nineteenth century into the twentieth century and was often used for mid-week Lenten services. The Common Service of 1888 had restored Matins and Vespers to Lutheran service books in North America, and various Protestant religious orders and houses, principally in Europe, have developed forms of Daily Prayer for their own use that have been adopted by others as well.

In the Roman Catholic Church, the 1568 Breviary of Pius V became the standard until the second third of the twentieth century. It somewhat simplified the medieval forms; the weekday *preces,* for example, were limited to Advent and Lent. The Psalter continued to be divided over one week. The breviary was still long and complicated with an abbreviated lectionary, and it was widely received as an onerous duty rather than a joyful obligation. The Second Vatican Council therefore initiated a thorough-going revision of the Office with notable goals: (1) Lauds and Vespers are the most important offices of the day, the "two hinges on which the Office turns"; (2) Matins is to be revised with an emphasis on the readings so that it can be said at any time of the day; (3) Prime is suppressed, and only one of the "little hours" during the daytime need be said; (4) Compline is to be clearly the prayer at the end of the day; (5) the Psalter is to be distributed over a period longer than one week; (6) the lectionary is to be revised so the readings are longer and the patristic readings are in accordance with historical facts; (7) the selection of hymns is to be expanded; (8) the offices are to be said at the appropriate time of the day, not saved up and prayed all at one time. The result of the revision, the *Liturgy of the Hours,* is a far more attractive Office, understood as the property of the whole church, laity as well as clergy. The revised structure still leans, however, toward a private and clerical form. Nonetheless, the basic principles have had wide impact on Western Christianity. The influence of the revised *Liturgy of the Hours* is seen in the forms of Daily Prayer in the 1978 *Lutheran Book of Worship,* the 1979 *Book of Common Prayer,* and the 1987 *Daily Prayer* (Supplemental Liturgical Resource 5) of the Presbyterian churches. Indeed, this ecumenical pattern is now shared by many Christian denominations.

Clearly, then, the forms of Daily Prayer offer us a way to move beyond our own sometimes narrow world as we pray, and to join hearts and voices with countless believers of time past and time to come.

4

With All God's Creatures

If, as we have seen, our practice of Daily Prayer links us with the church of every time and place in the praise of God, that still does not exhaust the ways in which our ordered prayer, this prayer for every day, takes us beyond ourselves. True, we join with all people in praising God. Yet the Creator was receiving praise long before human beings appeared on the scene. In our self-infatuation we often think that human beings alone are capable of understanding and therefore rendering appropriate praise. A humbling lesson we need to learn is deeply ingrained in the Bible as well as Christian tradition. The great hymn *Te Deum* ("You are God; we praise you," *LBW*, p. 139) sums up this understanding: "all creation worships you." One might take that to mean human beings, a poetic way of saying that everybody should worship God. But the phrase (in the original Latin it is *omnis terra veneratur*) means just what it literally says: all the earth, all creation, every aspect of the universe, every part of God's creation, all creatures. In English usage, reflecting the Latin origin of the word, anything that has been made is a "creature" made by the Creator—people and animals and birds and fish and trees and water and air and rocks and planets and moons and stars and time itself. Psalm 148 bids all of these creations to join in God's praise: "Let them praise the name of the LORD, for he commanded and they were created" (Ps. 148:5). All creation, all creatures, all created things worship the Creator.

This rich affirmation needs to be unpacked. And following the lead of the psalmists, many Christians have found poetic verse to be the ideal medium for prayers of praise. Hymns help us take our part with all of creation in the worship of God. Thus, they are an integral part of Daily Prayer. In these hymns, the beauty of the earth as a gift from God is a familiar idea, as in Folliott Sandford Pierpoint's stanza,

For the beauty of the earth,
For the beauty of the skies,
For the love which from our birth
Over and around us lies:
Christ, our Lord, to you we raise
This our sacrifice of praise. (*LBW* 561)

The hymn "Beautiful Savior" ("Fairest Lord Jesus") sings,

Fair are the meadows,
Fair are the woodlands,
Robed in flowers of blooming spring;
Jesus is fairer,
Jesus is purer,
He makes our sorrowing spirit sing. (*LBW* 518)

This familiar hymn notes the beauty of nature, but it does so in order to stress the surpassing beauty of Christ.

The praise of the beauty of the earth and sky moves quickly and naturally to praise of the Creator, whose beauty is revealed in the beauty and order of the world.

This is my Father's world;
The birds their carols raise;
The morning light, the lily white,
Declare their maker's praise.
This is my Father's world;
He shines in all that's fair.
In the rustling grass I hear him pass;
He speaks to me everywhere. (*LBW* 554)

In the translation of the *yigdal* from the Jewish liturgy by Max Landsberg and Newton M. Mann, "Praise to the Living God! All Praised Be His Name," the earth speaks the praise of its Creator.

Formless, all lovely forms declare his loveliness;
Holy, no holiness of earth can be express.
Lo, he is Lord of all. Creation speaks his praise,
And everywhere above, below, his will obeys. (*H82* 372)

Henry Van Dyke's "Joyful, Joyful We Adore Thee" finds in the works of nature an invitation to praise.

All thy works with joy surround thee,
*   Earth and heaven reflect thy rays,*
Stars and angels sing around thee,
*   Center of unbroken praise.*
Field and forest, vale and mountain,
*   Flowery meadow, flashing sea,*
Chanting bird and flowing fountain
*   Call us to rejoice in thee.*   (*LBW* 551)

The whole earth is full of God's glory, as Isaiah heard (Isaiah 6:3; see also Jeremiah 23:24b; Psalm 24:1, 50:12, 72:19; Wisdom 1:7; Sirach 43:27; Colossians 1:16) and as Christians sing in the Sanctus at the celebration of the Eucharist: "Holy, holy, holy Lord, God of power and might: Heaven and earth are full of your glory." The cosmos is filled with beauty. Wherever we look, we see the hand of the Creator, the signature of the mighty Maker.

Moreover, a principal characteristic of the Creator, recognized in many hymns, is loving care of what has been created.

Your bountiful care, what tongue can recite?
It breathes in the air; it shines in the light;
It streams from the hills, it descends to the plain,
And sweetly distills in the dew and the rain. (*LBW* 548)

In the biblical picture, God shows concern not only for human beings but for animals and vegetation as well. God chides Jonah, "You are concerned about the bush . . . . And should I not be concerned about Nineveh, that great city, in which there are more than a hundred and twenty thousand persons . . . and also many animals?" (Jonah 4:10–11). And in the New Testament Jesus testified to God's concern even for the sparrow (Matt. 10:29; Luke 12:6). God's all-embracing concern extends to the minutest constituents of the cosmos, and those elements, in their own way, can respond to this care and offer praise.

A hymn from the Greek additions to the book of Daniel makes the cosmic praise more specific. *Benedicite, omnia opera* ("All You Works of the Lord"—LBW 18), like Psalm 148, invites praise *from the cosmic order* (angels and all powers of the Lord, heavens and waters above the heavens, sun, moon, and stars, rain and dew, winds, fire, and heat, winter and summer, dew and snow, frost and cold, ice and sleet, nights and days, light and darkness, clouds and thunderbolts); *from the earth and its creatures* (mountains and hills, vegetation, springs, seas, and streams, whales and all that move in the waters, birds, beasts, flocks and herds, men and women); *from the people of God* (priests and servants of God, spirits and souls of the righteous, the holy and humble). All are called upon to praise and glorify the Lord forever.

Psalm 150, the grand doxology that brings the Psalter to a ringing close, invites "everything that breathes" to praise the Lord. One might at first think of all people and other breathing animals and birds and fish. But the psalm lists trumpets, lutes, harps, tambourines, strings, pipes, and cymbals. Some musical instruments obviously have breath, for trumpets and pipes are given life by human breath blowing through them. But the psalm also mentions other instruments not given life by breath from human lungs. Musical instruments have their own voice, their own "breath" that is released when human fingers and hands set them in motion, plucking the strings of a lute or harp, shaking a tambourine, clashing cymbals together. All that grand racket—for such was the accompaniment of the psalms—rises in praise of the Lord.

All these depend on human hands and skill. Other psalms extend this understanding of intentional praise to include the works of nature as well. Psalm 114, in Christian use associated with Easter, in Jewish use associated with the Exodus from Egypt, declares that

> *When Israel came out of Egypt, . . .*
> *The sea beheld it and fled;*
> *Jordan turned and went back.*
> *The mountains skipped like rams,*
> *and the little hills like young sheep.*(*BCP* 756–7, *LBW* 271)

The waters and the dry land saw and responded to the formative act of deliverance, running and skipping and frolicking. It is a delightfully vigorous picture. Isaiah has a similar picture of the rejoicing of creation:

> Sing, O heavens, for the Lord has done it;
>   shout, O depths of the earth;
> break forth into singing, O mountains,
>   O forest, and every tree in it!
> For the Lord has redeemed Jacob,
>   and will be glorified in Israel. (Isa. 44:23)

In Job 38:7 we learn that in celebration of the creative actions, "the morning stars sang together." Later understanding tamed the notion and made the stars into a metaphor for angels, and so at the new creation Luke has the chorus of angels sing when Christ was born, echoing and renewing the praise when the world was first made. In a view maintained more consistently in the Christian East than in the West, the whole cosmos is able to know that it has been raised to a new plane of existence. It is not that one assigns human emotions to nature, but that the whole cosmos as a dynamic, living unity is able to praise and even to love its Lord, who is its creator and redeemer.

Nature is never quiet. A young man from the city driving into the country on a summer evening with his car windows open remarked, "It is so noisy in the country! The city has horns, sirens, buses, but you know that each of these noises will soon be over, replaced by others. But in the country the din never stops, even at night. The insects keep up their continual racket all through the night." And so they do, singing out their brief span of life before cool weather sets in and their life is buried in the bark of trees until spring releases the life of the next generation.

One of the delights of nature is the song of birds. Luther, although his mind was preoccupied with other things, remarked the joyful vigor of the birds while he was in hiding in the Wartburg, "in the land of the birds," translating the Bible into German. He often made reference to birds in his writing and conversation. Lecturing on Psalm 84:3 he considers the meanings of "nest" and remarks, "who would have looked for so great a mystery in the most ordinary activity of birds?" (LW 11:142). In considering the verse Luther reveals that he is an interested observer of nature. Most impressively, in his lectures on the Sermon on the Mount (Matt. 6:26) he calls the birds our "schoolmasters and teachers": "Their living example is an embarrassment to us." We hear their great multitude singing and preaching every day, but we pay no attention. They sing Matins and Lauds to their Lord early in the morning before they eat "although none knows of a single grain laid away in store," Luther says. They sing a lovely Benedicite and leave their cares to God. Indeed, Luther declares, God enjoys it when "the dear little birds" fly around and sing without a care in the world because they trust completely God's goodness to supply all their needs.

Mortals alone of all creation are out of step, and so "a little finch . . . is [our] theologian and master in the Scriptures" (LW 21:197–8).

Animals that make few sounds nonetheless express their joy by their active life: deer bounding through the woods, white tails flashing like flags, squirrels busy gathering their hoard, hawks soaring for hours in sheer delight on currents of air. Nature is vigorously alive, and the closer to it we are able to live, the more we know of the richness of its life and praise.

We must beware of romanticizing nature, for it is not all a pleasant and joyful picture. The natural world, like humanity, is fallen as Genesis 3 describes, corrupted by human sin and therefore, as Tennyson described it, "red in tooth and claw" (*In Memoriam* liv).

Nonetheless, in the biblical view nature is not a thing that humans are free to use, despoil, alter at will. Humans are creatures living beside other animals, existing together with all other living things and the air we breathe and the water that supports our life. The natural world is not an inanimate thing but a web of living creatures whose lives all delicately interconnect with one another making us all interdependent in one organic whole. We cannot disrupt one part, for example exterminating one species of bird, without shaking the whole web and damaging the delicate balance on which all of us creatures depend. Rachel Carson's classic book of 1962, *Silent Spring,* warned against the dangers of insecticides. The title suggests a deeply frightening image: springtime without the joyful sounds of new life, the loss of countless choristers who would otherwise be singing the Creator's praise.

St. Francis of Assisi understood that nature as God's creation is not our mother, as the traditional label would have it, but rather our sister. We and all nature are members of one large and complex family, formed by the Maker of all things, visible and invisible, seen and unseen. St. Francis in his *Canticle of the Creatures,* known in William H. Draper's translation as "All Creatures of Our God and King," invited all the elements of the natural world to praise their Creator: beginning with sun and the moon and moving through the members of our cosmic family (wind and clouds, morning and evening, water and fire, earth and vegetation, everyone of tender heart). Even death is instructed to praise God. The whole life cycle of all nature is a great act of praise to God who made it and who orders it all.

Not only are humanity, animals, and birds moved to praise their Maker. Indeed, the earth itself—flowers and trees and all growing things, the sky and the air and the winds, clouds and crisp autumn days with their invigorating clarity, night and day and the annual turning of the seasons—offers praise. At the crucifixion, nature itself recoiled from the agony of the death of its God. The passion accounts in the gospels tell of the darkness that descended at noon on Good Friday and of the earthquake that shattered the tombs, and Christian hymnody has elaborated the theme. Gregory the Great (540–604) sang to Christ (in Ray Palmer's translation of the hymn, "O Christ Our King, Creator, Lord"),

Thou didst create the stars of night,
Yet thou hast veiled in flesh thy light . . .

When thou didst hang upon the tree
The quaking earth acknowledged thee,

When thou didst there yield up thy breath,
The world grew dark as shades of death.(SBH 62)

That profound and mystical insight continued through the Reformation. The Nonconformist hymnwriter Isaac Watts (1674–1748) mused in his hymn "Alas, and Did My Savior Bleed,"

Well might the sun in darkness hide
And shut his glories in
When God, the mighty maker, died
For his own creatures' sin.(LBW 98)

When the darkness was ended, nature rang out in joy in response to the resurrection. Venantius Fortunatus' great Easter hymn *Salve festa dies*, "Welcome, Festival Day!" understands the renewal of nature in the spring (in the northern hemisphere) as nature's share in greeting, proclaiming, and participating in the resurrection:

Earth her joy confesses, clothing her for spring,
all fresh gifts returned with her returning King:
bloom in every meadow, leaves on every bough,
speak his sorrow ended, hail his triumph now.
Months in due succession, days of lengthening light,
hours and passing moments praise thee in their flight.

Brightness of the morning, sky and fields and sea,
Vanquisher of darkness, bring their praise to thee.(*H82* 179)

The natural world responds with joy to the resurrection of Christ, whose victory over death renewed the world of nature as well as all humanity.

The understanding continued in certain hymns. Johann Mentzer (1658–1734) in the hymn "Oh, that I Had a Thousand Voices" wrote,

You forest leaves so green and tender
    That dance for joy in summer air,
You meadow grasses, bright and slender,
    You flowers so fragrant and so fair,
    You live to show God's praise alone.
    Join me to make his glory known!

All creatures that have breath and motion,
    That throng the earth, the sea, the sky,
Come, share with me my heart's devotion,
    Help me to sing God's praises high!
    My utmost powers can never quite
    Declare the wonders of his might! (*LBW* 560)

The psalm prayer for Psalm 98 given in *LBW: Minister's Edition* prays to the Holy Trinity, "As the seas roar and the hills sing together, we too will praise you for your great triumph." The psalm prayer to Psalm 96, echoing verses 11–13, begins, "Lord Jesus, the incarnate Word, when you consented to dwell with us, the heavens were glad and the earth rejoiced." The cosmos responds to its Creator with praise.

"Take words with you and return to the LORD," says the prophet Hosea (14:2). Human beings use words, and this suggests a unique relationship with God. In many ways this is our distinctive gift. We believe that we, of all creation, are most capable of communicating with God. A basic biblical concept declares the highest form of communication to be words. It was by speaking words that God created the universe: God said, "Let there be light," and creation began. The Creator spoke the universe into being. Last of all (according to the order of events in the first chapter of Genesis) human beings were created and, as the crown of creation, given dominion and mastery over every other living thing. Moreover (according to the order of events in the second chapter of Genesis), people were given authority to name the animals, and in the biblical world knowing a name gives one power over what is thus named. Finally, in the third chapter of Genesis, after the fall, the Creator talks with the man and the woman, and they respond to him. God converses with human beings, something that does not occur during any other part of creation. God talks to the serpent, but the serpent is not given a chance to reply. God only commands and punishes the instigator of rebellion. Human beings alone are permitted conversation with the Creator.

The gift of language is also our great responsibility. The rest of creation is wordless. Even birds with their joyful and expressive songs, whales with their communicative sounds, dogs and cats with their vocabularies, even they do not have words and language as we know them. It is therefore the responsibility of human beings blessed with the gift of language to express the praise for the rest of creation. We give of our treasure of language to make their wordless praise complete. A thought that rises in our minds is incomplete until we find words to form and express that thought to others. So the wordless praise of creation may be understood to be incomplete without the addition of human speech to give it full expression.

There is a further dimension of our relationship to the praise of all creation, one that begins to draw us back to the rhythms of Daily Prayer. Psalm 19 asserts that "the heavens are telling the glory of God; and the firmament proclaims his handiwork." The succession of days "pours forth speech, and night to night declares knowledge." But, the psalm says, this praise is without words: "There is no speech, nor are there words; their voice is not heard." The praise of the skies, darkness and light, is wordless, and yet it is effective. Their inaudible voice goes out through all the earth. There are, we are reminded, other kinds of speech than spoken and written words, and such symbolic speech can have great power. "Their [silent] voice goes out through all the earth, and their [unspoken] words to the end of the world." The expression of the cosmos, because it transcends human language, can be heard and understood by all of humankind. Such a truly ecumenical voice is like the voice of the church speaking through all the languages of earth and uniting those who otherwise cannot understand one another, as the story of the Day of Pentecost (Acts 2) describes.

The psalm prayer to Psalm 136 asks, "Listen to the song of the universe, the hymn of resurrection, sung by your Church." The prayer to Psalm 148 prays, "Accept creation's hymn of praise from our lips, and let the praise that is sung in heaven resound in the heart of every creature on earth." Humans supply words to the voice of all creation. Put more forcefully, our words are necessary for the fullness of creation's praise.

The angels, those creatures that trouble rational minds but stir our imaginations, rejoice perpetually in the presence of the Triune God. They have witnessed the divine plan of salvation from its very beginning in heaven through all of its course on earth, and without interruption they proclaim their praise. St. John the Divine describes the scene.

> The four living creatures [the first like a lion, the second like an ox, the third with a face like a human face, and the fourth like a flying eagle], each of them with six wings, are full of eyes all around and inside. Day and night without ceasing they sing,
> > "Holy, holy, holy,
> > the Lord God the Almighty,
> > who was and is and is to come. " (Rev. 4:8)

Their unceasing song, rooted in the vision of Isaiah (6:2–3), and echoing the fantastic imagery of Ezekiel (1:5, 10), merges the old covenant and the new and unites the heavenly praise in one endless song.

The church on earth, aware of its linguistic limitation, asks the assistance of the angelic choirs, seeking to join mortal voices with the songs of the heavenly hosts. The hymn "Hail, Thou Once Despised Jesus," in the revision in the *Hymnal 1982*, pleads,

> *Help, ye bright angelic spirits,*
> > *All your noblest anthems raise;*
> *Help to sing our Savior's merits,*
> > *Help to chant Emmanuel's praise!* (*H82* 495)

Henry Francis Lyte's familiar paraphrase of Psalm 103, "Praise, My Soul, the King of Heaven," makes a similar request but expands it to include an invocation of the sun and moon and all creatures that dwell with us in time and space:

> *Angels, help us to adore him;*
> > *Ye behold him face to face;*

Sun and moon, bow down before him,
  Dwellers all in time and space.
    Alleluia, alleluia!
  Praise with us the God of grace. (*H82* 410)

In the Eucharist, the purpose of the Preface of the Great Thanksgiving is to join the earthly church's praise with the praise of "angels and archangels and all the company of heaven," uniting our praise and prayer with theirs. Daily Prayer is another expression of that same desire. It joins mortals with the unceasing song of the choirs of heaven and with the joyful though wordless song of all of God's creation.

We join the angels' song, but most of all we join in the prayer of Christ the High Priest. Christians are taught to pray "through Jesus Christ our Lord," who is divine and human, the "mediator between God and humankind" (1 Tim. 2:5). Christians also join Christ's perpetual intercession for the world and pray with him as well as through him. In the Christian understanding, Christ is the focus and conduit of all praise.

Dulled by sin, we cannot always see the glory of God pervading the entire cosmos. We cannot always hear the songs of heaven. Shakespeare had Lorenzo, a gentleman of Venice, lament,

  Look, how the floor of heaven
  Is thick inlaid with patens of bright gold.
  There's not the smallest orb which thou behold'st
  But in his motion like an angel sings,
  Still choiring to the young-eyed cherubins.
  Such harmony is in immortal souls,
  But whilst this muddy vesture of decay
  Doth grossly close it in, we cannot hear it.
                  (Merchant of Venice V.i.58–65)

Daily Prayer helps us to see through the cracks in our prison walls, to glimpse the outside world in all its splendor, to push back the horizon, and to join even now the eternal songs of heaven, in anticipation of the final day.

A teaching of the Catholic faith especially clear in Eastern Orthodoxy is the idea of *theosis,* the divinization of humanity. Athanasius (*On the Incarnation* 54) put it in a stunning formulation: God was humanized so that we might be divinized. God became human

so that humans might become divine. Still more dazzling is the divinization not only of humanity but of the whole cosmos as well. All creatures
will be purified and transformed in that glorious end time when at last
God will be "all in all" (1 Cor. 15:28). In the face of such promises
human understanding cracks, and in our humility only adoration will
survive.

In their worship, in their prayer, Christians anticipate the praise of
God by the chorus of all creatures singing together in a renewed world.
The praise of God belongs to the joy of a perfection granted by the
Creator and Redeemer. We have not yet attained that perfection, to be
sure, but the community, in fact all creation, is assured a share in the
glory that has already appeared in Christ. The praise is now said by a
few, but it is done for all as an anticipation and promise of the future
fulfillment and consummation.

5
Words Rise to Song

Prayer is not just ordinary conversation; it is focused speech. Indeed, prayer is more than uttered words. Whenever words are accompanied by emotion and deep feeling, they rise above mundane speech and take on a rhythm that gives increased force to their sound, and the rhythm rises into melody and song.

When we are happy, we sing. A broad smile is not enough when our spirit is filled with a great joy. Ordinary words will not suffice. We require something higher, grander, more joyful than usual. We hum strains of gladness; we even break into song, rising above the confines of usual speech, for only the best sounds we know—words combined with rhythm and melody and music—are adequate to our feeling.

Jonathan Edwards, the brilliant American theologian and preacher, describes an emotion that he was not alone in experiencing.

My sense of divine things gradually increased, and became more and more lively, and had more of that inward sweetness. The appearance of everything was altered; there seemed to be, as it were, a calm, sweet cast, or appearance of divine glory, in almost every thing. God's excellency, his wisdom, his purity, and love, seemed to appear in every thing; in the sun, moon, and stars; in the clouds, and blue sky; in the grass, flowers, trees; in the water, and all nature; which used greatly to fix my mind. I often used to sit and view the moon for continuance; and in the day, spent much time in viewing the clouds and sky, to behold the sweet glory of God in these things; in the mean time, singing forth, with a low voice, my contemplations of the Creator and Redeemer. . . . I felt God, so to speak, at the first appearance of a thunder storm; and used to take the opportunity, at such times, to fix myself in order to view the clouds, and see the lightnings play, and hear the majestic and awful voice of God's thunder, which oftentimes was exceedingly entertaining, leading me to sweet contemplations of my great and glorious God. While thus engaged, it always seemed natural to me to sing, or chant for my meditations; or, to speak my thoughts in soliloquies with a singing voice.(*Personal Narrative*)

Even that stern and eloquent Calvinist found song inescapable in voicing his response to the power and beauty of God. As we are moved to God's praise, words begin to flow more elegantly than usual, and they rise through rhythm and meter into melody and song as we chant God's praise.

Poetry has always been at the center of Daily Prayer as it has been practiced through the centuries. The Psalms are at the heart of Jewish and Christian forms of prayer, and even in translation we can still hear and feel their poetry. It is a poetry different from the kind we are familiar with in English. It has a different kind of rhyme, not a repetition of similar sounds (*moon, June, tune,*) but a repetition of similar or related ideas. As can be seen in examples from Psalm 1, it is usually in two-line couplets. the first line stating an idea, *the second line repeating it* ("Therefore the wicked will not stand in the judgment,/nor sinners in the congregation of the righteous") *or restating it* ("their delight is in the law of the LORD,/and on his law they meditate day and night") *or expanding it* ("Happy are those who do not follow the advice of the wicked,/or take the path that sinners tread") *or sometimes giving the other side of the picture* ("for the LORD watches over the way of the righteous,/but the way of the wicked will perish").

The Psalter, "the hymnbook of the second temple," has always been a principal resource for Jewish and Christian worship. Even when the New Testament is printed separately, the psalms are often included with it as the one essential part of the Old Testament for Christian use. Jesus, a typical Jew, loved the psalms and frequently quoted them and referred to them, letting them speak for him, most notably on the cross (his only dying words according to Mark's account of the crucifixion), "My God, my God, why have you forsaken me?" (Psalm 22:1). The young church made use of the psalms in its teaching and life. Peter, after the suicide of Judas, used Psalm 69:25 and 109:8 as justification for the selection of a successor to restore the number of apostles to twelve.

In Protestant practice another kind of religious poetry became important for worship and devotion, even rivaling the place of the psalms. One of the great gifts of Lutheranism to Christian worship is the vernacular hymn. Hymns had been sung in Christian worship since early times, but with the Reformation they became the common property of the entire church, not only sung in worship but used in family devotion and private prayer as well. Sometimes they were read as devotional poetry, allowing the rhythmic words to speak apart from and undistracted by the supporting melody; but when possible, hymns were sung in homes.

Music is an essential, inescapable component of prayer (Col. 3:16). It has not always been clearly present, but it is always there, recognized or not. The psalms were the principal part of the late medieval breviaries. The entire Psalter was read through each week, and hymn texts were included also to be read as part of each office. Poetry and music are natural components of prayer.

The Holy Spirit teaches us how to sing the praise of God, and for Luther (*WA* 1:162; 6:218) the song of praise is an act of receiving rather than giving, a mark of the heavenly life joining the church on earth with the church in heaven. Only in hell, where there is no salvation, is the song of praise not heard. Faith, ultimately a gift of God, is an offering of praise, so human confession and praise are signs that we have received, accepted, and share the work of God.

Luther wrote in 1530 to Louis Senfl that those who are not moved by music are like stumps of wood and blocks of stone.

> For we know that music, too, is odious and unbearable to the demons. Indeed I plainly judge, and do not hesitate to affirm, that except for theology there is no art that could be put on the same level with music, since except for theology [music] alone produces what otherwise only theology can do, namely, a calm and joyful disposition. Manifest proof [of this is the fact] that the devil, the creator of saddening cares and disquieting worries, takes flight at the sound of music almost as he takes flight at the word of theology. This is the reason why the prophets did not make use of any art except music; when setting forth their theology they did it not as geometry, but as arithmetic, not as astronomy, but as music, so that they held theology and music most tightly connected, and proclaimed truth through Psalms and songs.
>
> (*LW* 49:428; see also 54:129–130)

Joy and jubilation are the dominant tones of the worship of God, the *cantus firmus* of preexisting melody to which are added our individual notes and harmonies.

The attention sometimes given to the prelude introducing the singing of hymns is a characteristic feature of Lutheran worship in many places, as is the practice of *alternation* in rendering hymns, allowing the organ or other instrument alone to speak a stanza of a hymn while the congregation listens, or the custom of sitting to listen to the playing of a postlude. In that tradition, music is regarded as part of the whole expression of worship, inseparable from the congregation's worship. A spoken service without any singing is almost unknown in Lutheran and Orthodox churches.

Sight and sound, words and silence, speaking and singing, single voices and the congregation, human voices and instruments interact in complex ways to engage our whole being and to entice us to greater praise. There is a regular rhythm in the construction and words of Daily Prayer that influences our spirit, speaking a language beyond logic in which words live not so much because of their rational content as by virtue of their sound and rhythm. Periods of prayer punctuate the day, giving it a shape and form and rhythm.

The Eucharist has a clear and identifiable goal, moving from gathering to listening, to the proclamation of the Word of God, to taking and blessing and sharing the bread of heaven and cup of salvation, to dispersing to serve God in the world. Even though the Eucharist is repeated every week, and in some places even daily, it has a linear shape following a definite and logical line from beginning to end. Daily Prayer, in contrast, is characterized by a circle, a regular and even unceasing repetition and with that a certain lack of specific direction and end. Its only purpose is praise, joining and sharing the songs of all creation. No wonder it seems "useless" to the modern world. From an impatient and goal-oriented world that wants to see things happen, Daily Prayer lifts us to another kind of time beyond the pressures of purpose and end, a timelessness of relaxation and pure pleasure.

The rhythm of such ordered prayer derives from the basic rhythms of the cosmos. It ties us to and echoes in us the daily rhythm of night and day, sunset and sunrise, darkness and light, recollection and rebirth, dying and rising, and it involves more distant echoes of the repetition of week after week, the turning of the seasons, and the cycles of the years.

It is a kind of mantra, untranslatable into a language other than its own, a rhythm like the pulse, the heartbeat of devotion (*LW* 24:89). It rises, finally, to elude all human powers of observation, description, and thought. That which words and reason cannot reach is touched by music, for music can see the invisible and understand the incomprehensible.

George Herbert (1593–1633), priest of the Church of England, poet, and accomplished musician, observed,

> *A verse may find him, who a sermon flies,*
> *And turn delight into a sacrifice.* ("The Church Porch" 5–6)

There is a seductiveness about rhythm and melody that can engage us as can nothing else. Sir Philip Sidney, in a widely influential definition, said that the purpose of poetry was to teach and to delight. Herbert expands that definition, for, he asserts, poetry has the power to transform pleasure into a religious act, changing self-centeredness into self-giving. The closely related arts of poetry and music are essential in the practice of religion. They take earthly experience and redirect it to more exalted purposes, lifting to God what is ours and laying it before the throne for God's use and praise and service.

6

Praying in Daily Life

The people of God must find time for prayer each day. The Eucharist provides nourishment for our journey through the world, feeding us weekly, or at least regularly, with the bread of heaven, giving us a foretaste of the feast to come. But the Holy Communion needs to be supported and supplemented by the daily seeking of God to bind us to the basic rhythm of creation and re-creation: "evening and morning, sunset and dawning" (*LBW* 465). Daily prayer acknowledges the pulse beating within us and in all the cosmos.

Daily prayer requires discipline, and that is often an unwelcome requirement. Discipline may suggest a rigid legalism that denies or postpones pleasure in order to try to live up to someone else's notion of what is good for us. And, in a time of intense individualism, that seems an outmoded and destructive confinement.

We are, however, beginning to see the results of living for oneself alone, in pursuit of immediate gratification from whatever may entice us without restriction or responsibility of discipline. Often to our pain we then learn that we cannot have it all. The fruitful life is the disciplined life. The seventeenth-century English priest and poet George Herbert, who knew a good bit about prayer, likened our life to a garden that requires careful and constant pruning to gain strength and healthy growth.

I bless thee, Lord, because I GROW
Among thy trees, which in a ROW
To thee both fruit and order OW.

What open force, or hidden CHARM
Can blast my fruit, or bring me HARM,
While the inclosure is thine ARM?

51

Inclose me still for fear I START.
Be to me rather sharp and TART,
Then let me want thy hand and ART.

When thou dost greater judgments SPARE
And with thy knife but prune and PARE,
Ev'n fruitful trees more fruitful ARE.

Such sharpness shows the sweetest FREND:
Such cuttings rather heal than REND:
And such beginnings touch their END.

The title of this "pruning poem," significantly, is "Paradise." John Milton in *Paradise Lost* presents a similar understanding of the fruitfulness of obedience. Eve in the garden of paradise, just before the Fall, remarks to Adam that their work in the garden "under our labor grows,/Luxurious by restraint" (IX.208–209). Discipline and restraint make life—human life as well as vegetative life—abundant, fruitful, and satisfying.

Discipline is healthful, but it does not produce results quickly or easily. It is a gradually rewarding process. Prayer requires us to establish space between ourselves and the pressures and demands of the world that so easily overwhelm us. We are called to be separate from the cultural values that are often destructive of traditional spirituality. If we are to live such a life by ourselves, on our own, we will no doubt fail. We need help. We need the comfort and encouragement of knowing that we are part of a tradition and a community embodying the struggle. Monasteries remind those deeply immersed in secular affairs of another way of being in the world. They can be a sign to us of the importance of paying attention to God and to what God is doing throughout creation.

There lies deep in certain people a suspicion of prayers from a book. Prayer must be from the heart, we insist; we must pray with feeling. To be sure, the best prayer is heart-felt and springs from the deepest recesses of one's being, but such deep and meaningful conversation is not always possible. A legitimate motive for prayer is sheer obedience: we pray because we as God's priestly people are expected to pray, are obliged to pray. Such a simple sense of duty is honorable and not to be despised. Luther, while commending "spiritual and sincere prayer," allowed, "there is such a great measure of grace in the word of God that even a prayer that is spoken with the mouth and without devotion (with a sense of obedience) becomes fruitful and irritates the devil" (*LW* 42:20).

In order to give the greatest benefit, the discipline of Daily Prayer needs to be carried out whether we feel like it or not, whether our heart is in it or not. For in such regular and dependable repetition lie the seeds of meaning for us, which can break open with new and unexpected life when we least expect it. But we must keep on doing our duty in times of spiritual dryness as well as in times of spiritual exultation to ready the ground for such sudden growth. Revelation comes to those who, like the shepherds abiding in the field outside Bethlehem, were just going faithfully and dependably about their daily duty.

Those who seek to develop a life of prayer, remembering the necessity of discipline and the restraint that produces luxurious growth, need to bind themselves to a *pattern of prayer* suitable to their own particular circumstances. Such a pattern should include five elements.

First, one needs to find or make a regular time, even if it must be brief, for prayer, especially in the evening and in the morning.

Second, one must spend time reading and meditating on the Scripture. In private devotion as our forebears sometimes practiced it, the daily memorization of a verse of Scripture not only encouraged them to make that verse their own for a day, but also encouraged them to give themselves to that verse, to shape and conform their conduct by it, to transform their lives by it. Such use of a brief passage of Scripture can assist us in being faithful to our calling to be God's people in the world.

Third, a pattern of prayer may include regular self-examination with confession and resolution to amend one's life.

Fourth, there must be a course of intercession for the needs of those dear to us, our pastors, political and governmental leaders, the world, those around us whom we know to be in need, and those forgotten ones who have no one to pray for them. The list of concerns for the Prayers in the Eucharist suggests the scope of one's own intercessions: the whole church, the nations, those in need, the parish, special concerns. One day of the week could be dedicated to a particular area of concern: Sunday, for example, the unity of the church; Monday, the clergy and other ministers; Tuesday, the nations; Wednesday, peace; Thursday, those in need; Friday, special concerns; Saturday, the parish.

Fifth, a rule of prayer should include training oneself in offering silent prayers, intercessions, and thanksgivings throughout the day as occasion suggests, making use of time usually wasted, such as waiting at traffic lights, to encourage and foster the practice of the presence of God.

Those who adopt such a pattern will need regularly to renew their intention, for the temptation to quit is strong. Do not look for obvious and prompt results even though such an attitude is contrary to the prevailing modern spirit. Our prayer is an offering to God, who will use our sacrifice in ways beyond our perception and understanding. To know that we join in the perpetual intercession of Christ on behalf of the world is sufficient reward.

Use the riches of Daily Prayer as a guide, and shape your devotional life by the ancient pattern that binds our praise to the choirs of heaven and to all the works and creatures of the natural world. As song joins us to a large and even unimagined unity of praise, so does the cycle of Daily Prayer. Regular prayer in the evening and in the morning—with others if at all possible, but if not, then individually—can open our eyes to dimensions of the chorus of praise we never before even suspected. In our regular and unceasing pattern of prayer, we echo the ancient pattern of Genesis: evening and morning, prayer as the night falls and a waiting through the darkness for the first signs of a new day of grace and promise "as earth rolls onward into light," as John Ellerton's hymn "The Day Thou Gavest, Lord, Has Ended" puts it.

The exploration and use of Daily Prayer is a productive place to begin one's education in liturgy, its meaning, character, and symbolism. There we find the basic alternation of the world—darkness and light—used with great and profound effect. The acknowledgment and celebration of this alternation in Daily Prayer ties us to creation, to the movement of the solar system, to the experience of all living creatures. Moreover, it ties us, with modern Judaism, to ancient Israel, which continued the pattern and offered prayer in the evening and in the morning. Beyond that, Daily Prayer ties us to the experience of the death and resurrection of Christ and to the anticipation of our own death and resurrection. Night and day, bondage and freedom, death and resurrection are joined in one proclamation continuing without end.

In actual practice, what can busy people do? Here are seven suggested steps in developing a life of prayer.

First, begin modestly. Do not attempt too much initially so as not to become discouraged by not being able to keep up what you began.

Second, as the early church order the *Didache* (8) directs, pray the Lord's Prayer in the morning, at noon, and in the evening. This familiar prayer is not only a model prayer but is instruction in prayer as well, given in answer to the apostles' request, "Lord, teach us to pray." Luther, following in a long tradition of Christian teachers, took this basic prayer and uncovered great riches as he expounded it in his devotional commentary of 1519, *An Exposition of the Lord's Prayer for Simple Laymen* (*LW* 42:15–81). Think carefully about the words as you say them over and over, day after day. Let one phrase from the prayer rise to your conscious attention each time you say with confidence the words our Savior taught us.

Third, when you are ready for another step (don't rush things) memorize a prayer for the evening and a prayer for the morning to be used in addition to the Lord's Prayer. A classic evening prayer is the collect for peace used in Evening Prayer (Vespers) in the Lutheran and Anglican traditions:

> Most holy God, the source of all good desires, all right judgments, and all just works: Give to us, your servants, that peace which the world cannot give, so that our minds may be fixed on the doing of your will, and that we, being delivered from the fear of all enemies, may live in peace and quietness; through the mercies of Christ Jesus our Savior. (*BCP* 123)

Another useful prayer is the one Luther suggests for evening in his *Small Catechism:*

> We give thanks to you, heavenly Father, through Jesus Christ your dear Son, that you have this day so graciously protected us. We beg you to forgive us all our sins and the wrong which we have done. By your great mercy defend us from all the perils and dangers of this night. Into your hands we commend our bodies and souls, and all that is ours. Let your holy angels have charge of us, that the wicked one have no power over us. (*LBW* 166)

A classic morning prayer is the collect for grace used in the Anglican and Lutheran forms of Morning Prayer (Matins):

> Lord God, almighty and everlasting Father, you have brought us in safety to this new day: Preserve us with your mighty power, that we may not fall into sin, nor be overcome by adversity; and in all we do, direct us to the fulfilling of your purpose; through Jesus Christ our Lord. (*BCP* 100)

Another prayer for morning is suggested by Luther in the *Small Catechism:*

> We give thanks to you, heavenly Father, through Jesus Christ your dear Son, that you have protected us through the night from all danger and harm. We ask you to preserve and keep us, this day also, from all sin and evil, that in all our thoughts, words, and deeds we may serve and please you. Into your hands we commend our bodies and souls and all that is ours. Let your holy angels have charge of us, that the wicked one have no power over us.
>
> *(LBW 163)*

When a prayer such as these has been memorized, it can then be prayed while one is going to or from work, or otherwise lightly occupied, and the words can be the source of devotional meditation.

Fourth, when you are ready for more, carry a Psalter with you. Read and ponder a psalm a day, then one in the evening and one in the morning. To guide you, use the psalm table in *Lutheran Book of Worship* (p. 178) or *The Book of Common Prayer* (pp. 936–1001) or use the division of the Psalter given in *The Book of Common Prayer* for monthly praying of the psalms (pp. 585–808).

Fifth, to continue your use of biblical songs learn the Gospel canticles for evening and for morning. Copy, carry with you, pray, and memorize the canticle for evening, *Magnificat,* the Song of Mary (Luke 1:46–55) and then the canticle for morning, *Benedictus,* the Song of Zechariah (Luke 1:68–79). Pray these songs after the psalms and conclude with a prayer and the Lord's Prayer. You are now using the basic core of Daily Prayer.

Sixth, read the Bible. Follow the daily lectionary given in *The Book of Common Prayer* (pp. 936–1001) or in *Lutheran Book of Worship* (pp. 179–192) or in *Christian Prayer* (pp. 2064–2071). Note that "Year 1" begins with the First Sunday in Advent *preceding* odd-numbered years; "Year 2" begins with the First Sunday in Advent preceding even-numbered years. (So, for example, Year 1 begins with Advent 1996, 1998, 2000, etc.) One need not use all three readings every day. Again, do not attempt too much. It is better to read with attention one lesson than to read two or three in haste.

Finally, when you are comfortable with the structured life of prayer, use more of Daily Prayer as the form of your prayer. It is important not to attempt too much at first. It is equally important not to be content with too little. No matter how small your beginning, work toward a goal; and that goal should be the use of Daily Prayer in as full a form as is possible in your situation. And, once more, it must be said that the ideal is to engage in Daily Prayer with other Christians.

If the people of God take the ancient forms of Evening and Morning Prayer as the basis for their own prayer, then their own efforts will be a less lonely activity. They will know that they are sharing in a large work embracing all times and all places and all creatures in the whole cosmos.

There is a core of Evening and Morning Prayer that ought to be recognizable in our daily prayer: a psalm, a passage of Scripture, the appropriate Gospel canticle (*Magnificat* in the evening, *Benedictus* in the morning), prayer and the Lord's Prayer. If such a pattern is identifiable in one's own individual or family prayer, then when several who follow such a course of prayer join together for prayer, such as at meetings in the congregation, the core can be elaborated: the psalm and the Gospel canticle can be sung, a hymn may be added following the psalm, a longer or a second passage of scripture may be read. When the congregation assembles for prayer, such as on weekdays during Advent, Lent, or Easter, further elaborations such as antiphons, responsories and further ceremonies can be added to the recognizable core that each member uses in private. In this way, there is a common shape giving unity, coherence, and continuity to the prayer of the people of God.

Those who share in the leadership of the church's liturgy—presiding and assisting ministers, pastors and deacons, clergy and laypeople—need to begin and to encourage the use of the services of Daily Prayer. These treasures lie undiscovered in most parishes. Those who minister in the house of God need first to commit themselves to the daily use of these historic forms, praying them each day with other members of the church staff and congregation or simply with their own families or even alone when there are no others who can join in. Daily Prayer reminds us that we are not alone when we pray and that one's praise is joined to that of all the universe.

The old medieval choir office with its roots deep in Jewish and Hebrew daily prayer is being restored as a service for the whole people of God because it possesses several characteristics to commend its use. (1) It is traditional. It maintains continuity with the past and establishes solidarity with others in the present. (2) It is elastic. It provides a form of prayer for use by an individual, by a few, by a large company. (3) It is continuous. It keeps the flame of prayer alive throughout the week and throughout the world, inviting us to join the ceaseless praise. (4) It is challenging. The work of prayer is seldom easy. It confronts us with ideas and attitudes that we may not feel or be aware of, disconcerting us but at the same time and by that very discontent affording an occasion and opportunity for growth. (5) It is honest. By fostering familiarity with the Word of God and with the response of our spiritual ancestors to that challenging word, Daily Prayer encourages honesty and openness, which characterized those who were not afraid to argue with God or to challenge the divine way of doing things. Those who learn to pray join with Abraham, Moses, and Jeremiah in confrontation with God's commands, and with Sarah in laughter at God's apparently preposterous plan, and with all the saints and believers through the ages who kept alive the old story that now has been entrusted to our care for preservation and transmission to those who come after us.

7

Pray without Ceasing

Historically, two means of setting forth the Christian experience of communion with God have been honored above all the rest: the Eucharistic meal and Daily Prayer. These two treasures of the church have not always been available to Christian people. Sometimes people were discouraged from sharing the Holy Communion and only watched while the priest assumed more and more exclusively the action of eating and drinking. Sometimes people were prevented from sharing the meal because it was celebrated (or *administered* or *observed* as the action was sometimes described) only a few times a year. Gradually, laypeople were prevented from sharing in the daily prayer of the Christian family as it continued to be available and prayed only in an increasingly unknown language and so increasingly prayed only by those who were required to learn that ancient language, the clergy. Daily Prayer was, in effect, although not necessarily in intention, removed from the hands and the hearts of the whole family of God and became more and more the property of the clerics. The churches of the Reformation attempted to restore the treasure of this prayer to the whole people of God. Matins and Vespers were for several centuries preserved in churches on the continent, usually as public services in the church buildings. The English church preserved something of the spirit of the ancient office by requiring its clergy to pray Morning Prayer and Evensong daily, in their parish churches when possible. The assumption clearly was that at least some of the people who were not required to do so might join in these services in the churches since they were in the vernacular language. During the seventeenth and eighteenth centuries there was in England a great outpouring of devotional books based on the ancient offices and in France there was a strong movement that created a host of local breviaries. Through changing taste and through deliberate suppression, these books fell into disuse during the past two centuries. Now again in an ecumenical age, interest is being shown in the Lord's Supper as the principal action of the Lord's Day and, to a lesser extent, in ordered forms of daily prayer.

Daily Prayer is a center providing stability, focus, and protection in times of crisis, an "anchor of the soul" (Heb. 6:19). In the historical experience of Israel and of Christian people, God has proved faithful and reliable, and Daily Prayer is a response to the divine acts of mercy and justice. The biblical experience was not neat and tidy but is the more convincing because, like all human experience, it was contradictory and ragged and confusing, and yet fascinating. The biblical experience is always forward-looking and future-directed, liberating humanity from the pretended securities of time and place and sending them forth on pilgrimage to find what it assures them is the real meaning of life. The biblical story is a history of movement and of passage: Abraham and Sarah passing from Ur to Canaan; Jacob from Canaan to Egypt; Moses and Israel from Egypt back to Canaan again; Jesus in pilgrimage from Galilee to Jerusalem; Paul from Jerusalem to Rome; and the young church from Rome to northern Europe and the New World, with other, more ancient movements passing to Asia and to Africa. A favorite Christian idea, from the writer to the Hebrews to John Bunyan to the Second Vatican Council, has seen the movement of God's people under the image of a pilgrimage. The early as well as the later emphasis has been on the corporate nature of the journey, for it is not a solitary trip that one must take, but a journey taken in company with others. It is the progress of the pilgrim people of God, of which all believers are a part. It is the task of the church's liturgy to celebrate this pilgrimage. The church's year, together with Daily Prayer, makes use of the movement of nature as a symbol of the movement of God's people: as day turns into darkness and darkness into day again and as the weeks and the seasons pass, the pilgrim people are that much closer to the goal for which all creation groans in travail. It is by keeping alive day by day, week by week, year by year the memory of the great things God has done that time is sanctified, recognized as the bearer of profound meaning, deeper still than the awe of primal people who charted the progress of the heavens and recorded the story of those beneath them.

Daily Prayer is a way of seeing life whole. It joins us to larger dimensions of time and space and, indeed, with the boundlessness of eternity.

It breaks us free from prisons of our own making and of our human limitations. It urges us toward the ever-receding horizon. The English priest and hymnwriter John Ellerton (1826–1893) expressed the inclusive and continuing spirit of the church's regulated devotion in a notable way.

The day, thou gavest, Lord, is needed,
*   the darkness falls at thy behest;*
to thee our morning hymns ascended,
*   thy praise shall sanctify our rest.*

We thank thee that thy Church, unsleeping
*   while earth rolls onward into light,*
through all the world her watch is keeping,
*   and rests not now by day or night.*

As o'er each continent and island
*   the dawn leads on another day,*
the voice of prayer is never silent,
*   nor dies the strain of praise away.*

So be it, Lord; thy throne shall never,
*   like earth's proud empires, pass away;*
thy kingdom stands, and grows forever,
*   till all they creatures own thy sway.* (*H82* 24)

Thus the church in Daily Prayer fulfills the admonition of Christ, who taught us to "pray always" (Luke 18:1), and of the Apostle who likewise charged the churches to "pray without ceasing" (1 Thess. 5:17).

The individual Christian must, of course, cease from prayer in order to work and sleep. In a sense, however, even these ordinary, mundane actions, when done in a spirit of trust and praise, can be themselves an effective prayer. *Laborare est orare,* said the monks: to work is to pray. And in the *Small Catechism* Luther provides prayers for use before and after eating, thus making each meal an act of praise. But the prayers and praises of Christians, who are part of the body of Christ, are never offered individually and alone. What Christians do—whether they are aware of it or not—is done in common with the rest of the people of God. One can view the continued prayer of the church rising in a splendid concert, and, as Ellerton said, while one part of the Church goes to sleep another is waking and taking up the ceaseless song. So, "as earth rolls onward into light," the grand and exquisite chain of praise is endlessly maintained.

The ordered devotion seeking to formulate this noble vision of unending praise is the church's Daily Prayer, a form of unceasing praise of God that is the chief purpose of Christian existence. It is the great anthem of perpetual praise and adoration and petition which the whole Christ, head and members, presents at every moment to the heavenly Father. It is the family prayer of the people of God, the breathing of the body of Christ. Together with the Eucharist, Daily Prayer is the choicest form of the church's praise and prayer.

The unceasing round of Daily Prayer is instructional, for it keeps fresh in the mind of the church, which employs it, the elementary facts of the Christian religion: what God has done for the world in the death and resurrection of Jesus of Nazareth. When Christian people order their devotional life according to the ancient pattern developed through the centuries, they are in effect enrolling in an advanced course in biblical dogmatic theology taught by the masters of the Christian tradition. They are having their souls stretched by some of the greatest spirits of Christendom as they take their place in the earthly choir that joins the celestial praise of the citizens of heaven.

The very act of remembering is, in the biblical understanding, a way of praise. We call to mind a great act of God—the Passover, for example—not just so that we will not forget it but also that we might be contemporary with it as the act comes out of the past to live in the present and to involve us in its power. Recollection is for edification and also for praise. These two purposes—praise and instruction—are joined in that "work of God" which builds up the body of Christ, Daily Prayer.

Until the third century, apparently, Morning Prayer and Evening Prayer were the public services in the meeting places of Christians, but a variety of writers commended prayer at each of the recognized dividing points of the day, and these regular times of prayer were soon invested with understandings that connected them with the actions of Jesus' passion. In this way, the church developed a means of consecrating the entire day to God. It was, ideally, pleasant and delightful rather than an arduous duty. The "hours" were times of refreshment in the desert of daily living, respites to revive drooping spirits.

The scheme grew increasingly elaborate and complex as more and more it became the exclusive property of monks and clergy. Although the call for reform of Daily Prayer went out before the Reformation divided the Western church, it has not yet been adequately acted upon. The plant that the church had taken five centuries to nurture had been allowed to grow untended for a thousand years. Its pruning and restoration could not be hurried. Now at last, the time seems right for Christians in many lands, evangelical as well as catholic, to join in the recovery of the form of prayer inherited from the early centuries of Christianity. Such a restored prayer ought surely to be a book making it possible for any Christian to participate in the common work of the whole people of God. These must be its characteristics: (1) Evening and Morning Prayer are the chief hours and are to be celebrated as such; (2) Daily Prayer is the property of all the people of God and ought to be shared by clergy and laity alike; (3) the purposes of Daily Prayer are to provide a scheme of regular and thorough Bible reading, to provide for the praying of the Psalter, and to provide prayers for the needs of the world.

In 1981, a study group of the North American Academy of Liturgy summarized the purpose of Daily Prayer with this statement: "The mystery of God in Christ is the center of the liturgy of the church. By celebrating Daily Prayer at certain times of the day which recall creation and re-creation, the church, gathered together in the Holy Spirit, hears the life-giving Word of God and in response to it voices the praise of creation, joins with the songs of heaven, shares in Christ's perpetual intercession for the world. This cycle of praise and prayer transforms our experience of time, deepening our understanding of how day and night can proclaim and celebrate the paschal mystery. Thus, the daily Liturgy of the Hours supplements and contrasts with the centrality of the Sunday Eucharist in the life of the church, edifying the one holy people of God until all is fulfilled in the kingdom of heaven."

Daily Prayer is a treasure waiting to be recovered, explored, and renewed. Developed largely in rural monastic settings and in, perhaps, less chaotic times, the regular course of praise and readings and prayer can still lift us to the presence of God. Daily Prayer invites us into that difficult existence that responds to and grasps and shares the love of God and bears the cost of the earnest spiritual life. The ancient cycle is unbroken still. Joined with God's people of all times and all place, with all the creatures, and with the whole choir of heaven, we are taken up to have our part in the unending song of praise that the bride offers to her Bridegroom in anticipation of the grand chorus of the renewed cosmos.